For my mom and dad

1/7/11

STARTED WORKING AT A NEW JOB TODAY. MET A
FEW INTERESTING PEOPLE. (SOME OF THEM ARE
FOREIGN-LOOKING.) THERE WAS THIS ONE GIRL
WHO SAID "HI" IN THE ELEVATOR. ALL I KNOW
ABOUT HER IS THAT:

① HER NAME IS **KELLY DONAHUE**.

② SHE SITS NEAR THE FAX MACHINE.

③ AND **I VOW TO PHYSICALLY DEFEAT HER IN A PHYSICAL FIGHT TO THE DEATH. PHYSICALLY!**

OH... NEW JOB HAS FREE COFFEE. I LIKE IT.

1/9/11

SO HERE'S A SKETCH/PROFILE OF THE ENEMY:

HEIGHT: 5'7-ish (?)
WEIGHT: NORMAL
GIRL WEIGHT

STRENGTHS: ATHLETIC,
ABLE TO
REPRODUCE
AND BREED
FUTURE
GENERATIONS
OF ENEMIES.

WEAKNESSES: T.B.D.

4/12/11

SAW KELLYR DONAHUE IN A CONFERENCE ROOM TODAY.
STARTED THINKING ABOUT WHAT I
COULD USE AS WEAPONS IF WE BOTH
GOT STUCK IN A CONFERENCE ROOM
AND "THE FIGHT" BEGINS.

→ POINTY
PENCIL FOR
EYE JABBING,
AND WRITING
ABOUT IT.

↑ SCISSORS FOR
STABBING,
AND/OR MORE
EYE JABBINGS,
AND/OR FIXING HER
AMISH HAIR-DO.

↘ PHONE CORD
FOR STRANGLING.

1/13/11

FIGHTING THE URGE TO YELL "YOU'RE DEAD!"
EVERY TIME I PASS BY KELLY DONAHUE.
THINK I MIGHT START CARRYING A BAGEL
AROUND SO IN CASE IT SLIPS OUT, I'LL
QUICKLY LOOK DOWN AT IT AND YELL
"YOU'RE BREAD!"

1/15/11

2:38 AM CAN'T SLEEP!
        THINKING ABOUT HOW
AWESOME IT'LL BE AFTER KICKING
KELLY DONAHUE'S ASS IN THE
ULTIMATE DEATH FIGHT TO THE DEATH.
'JAWS' IS PLAYING ON H.B.O.
WHERE CAN I GET A SHARK ???

1/23/11

I WAS DISCUSSING MY ~~DESIRE~~ NEED TO RID
THIS WORLD OF KELLY DONAHUE WITH MY
BUDDY GREG. HE DOESN'T KNOW KELLY DONAHUE
BUT HE TOO ~~WANTS~~ NEEDS ME TO ELIMINATE
HER FOR ONCE AND FOR ALL. GREG IS A
BLACK BELT IN [KRAV MAGA], THE
ISRAELI SELF DEFENSE FIGHTING STYLE
WHERE THEY USE WHATEVER'S AROUND
THEM TO ANNIHILATE THEIR ENEMY.
LIKE, IF THEY WERE EATING FALAFEL
NEAR AN ENEMY, THEY COULD PARALYZE
THEM WITH PITA BREAD. OR IF THEY
SPOTTED AN ENEMY WHILE INSIDE A
GUN & AMMO SHOP, THEY COULD ⟶

→ REMOVE ONE OF THE PRICE TAGS OFF
A REVOLVER AND GIVE THEIR ENEMY
A MILLION PAPER CUTS ON THEIR FINGER
WEBBINGS AND TONGUE UNTIL THEY
BLEED TO DEATH. SO WHAT I'm SAYING IS,
THIS IS TOTALLY GONNA GIVE ME TONS
OF NEW FUN WAYS TO MAKE
KELLY DONAHUE WISH SHE WAS NEVER
BORN AS KELLY DONAHUE.

I'VE BEGUN TO TAKE NOTICE OF DIFFERENT
PATTERNS IN KELLY DONAHUE'S ROUTINE.
THIS FOOLISH OVERSIGHT WILL LEAD TO
HER PAINFUL, BODY-CRUSHING DOWNFALL.

PATTERNS:

- GOES TO BATHROOM 4.2X A DAY.
  (PERFECT PLACE TO AMBUSH HER,
   HIDE BEHIND THE MAKE-UP COUNTER,
   OR THE BREASTMILKING STATION,
   OR WHATEVER ELSE GIRLS HAVE
   IN THEIR BATHROOMS.)

- AFTER SHE SNEEZES, SHE LOOKS AROUND
  TO SEE IF ANYONE IS THERE TO
  SAY "GOD BLESS YOU". SIGN OF WEAKNESS!

- TALKS ABOUT BEING ON A SUMMER VOLLEYBALL TEAM WAAAAY TO MUCH. THIS IS NOT SO MUCH A PATTERN THAT WILL HELP ME IN "THE FIGHT". IT IS SIMPLY ANOTHER EXAMPLE OF HOW GODDAMN ANNOYING SHE IS AND WHY THE UNITED NATIONS WILL SOON CREATE AN INTERNATIONAL HOLIDAY TO COMMEMORATE AND CELEBRATE THE DAY KELLY DONAHUE WAS REMOVED FROM EXISTENCE. (VIA DEATH.)

To: **Mark Svartz**

Cc:

Bcc:

Subject: **Silly Question**

From: Kelly Donahue/ ███████ 03:48 PM

Hey Mark,

Just curious, but were you going through my trash?

:)

-Kelly

1 | 30 | 11

SHE'S ONTO US !

BE MORE CAREFUL

2/6/11

SAW WHAT'S-HER-SMELL JAM UP THE
COPY MACHINE TODAY. KELLY DONAHUE
IS AS USELESS AS AN UMBRELLA TO
AN ARMLESS PERSON ON A NON-RAINY DAY.

2/10/11

I'M KINDA TORN ON HOW KELLY DONAHUE SHOULD
REACH HER ULTIMATE DEATH. EACH WAY
HAS ITS MERIT.

① PUNCHED TO DEATH:
  → PRO: SOOOO MUCH FUN
  → CON: MIGHT TAKE A WHILE

② ATTACKED BY TIGER:
  → PRO: MEMORABLE AND AWESOME
  → CON: GOTTA RENT/STEAL A TIGER

③ BURIED ALIVE:
  → PRO: EXTENDS HER ANGUISH
  → CON: I DON'T GET TO SEE
         HER MOMENT OF DEATH

→ (4) PUSHED INTO ONCOMING TRAFFIC:

    ↳ PRO: HIGH POTENTIAL FOR BROKEN BONES

    ↳ CON: MIGHT JUST LEAD TO INJURY,
            NOT DEATH (SUCKS!)

(5) POISONED:

    ↳ PRO: EASY

    ↳ CON: TOO EASY

(6) FATALLY WOUNDED BY HOLLYWOOD
ACTRESS DEMI MOORE:

    ↳ PRO: HOW AWESOME WOULD THAT BE?

    ↳ CON: DOES SHE DO THAT? (GOT A
          HUNCH SHE WOULD IF WE TELL
          HER ABOUT KELLY DONAHUE.)

7 SHOVED OFF A ROOFTOP:

↳ <u>PRO</u>: GET TO WATCH HER FALL

↳ <u>CON</u>: GOTTA FIND SOME CLEVER WAY OF TRICKING HER TO GO UP TO THE ROOF. (PROBABLY JUST TELL HER THEY PUT A VOLLEYBALL COURT UP THERE OR SOMETHING.)

8 STRANGLED BY HER OWN HAIR:

↳ <u>PRO</u>: NO WEAPON NEEDED

↳ <u>CON</u>: GOTTA TOUCH HER HAIR

2/14/11

NOTICED THAT KELLY DONAHUE DIDN'T HAVE ANY
FLOWERS OR GIFTS DELIVERED TO HER FOR
VALENTINE'S DAY. (OBVIOUSLY.)

SO I DECIDED TO GIVE HER

 THIS HERSHEY'S KISS ⇨

THAT I PAID

THIS RASTAFARIAN ⇨

TO BURY
IN HIS
MOLDY,
CRUSTY,
DREADLOCKS
FOR
60 SECONDS.

HAPPY VALENTINE'S DAY KELLY DONAHUE.
ENJOY THE MOUTH LICE.

2/22/11

HAPPY
BIRTHDAY
KELLY
DONAHUE.

FOR NOW.
YOU KNOW,
UNTIL YOU
LOSE THE
DEATH FIGHT
TO THE DEATH.

View Photos of Kelly (262)

Send Kelly a Message

Poke Kelly

Information

Birthday:
February 22

THANKS FOR
THE SUGGESTION,
FACEBOOK.

2/23/11

KELLY DONAHUE AND I GOT PUT ON THE SAME
PROJECT. DON'T KNOW HOW WELL THIS'LL WORK
OUT. EVERY TIME SHE LOOKS AT ME I
THINK SHE CAN TELL THAT "THE FIGHT"
IS ON MY MIND. AND IF KELLY DONAHUE
IS INDEED A MINDREADER, THEN HERE'S
A MESSAGE JUST FOR HER:

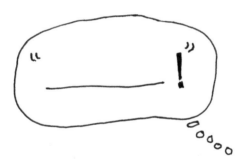

2/26/11

hooraykellydonahueisgonebywayo
fdeath.com is available! Just $10.69*

Select the domain names below that you would like to register:

Select All

	More Domain Options	
☑ hooraykellydonahueisgonebywayofdeath.com	$10.69*/yr	
☐ hooraykellydonahueisgonebywayofdeath.info	$0.89*	BEST VALUE!
☐ hooraykellydonahueisgonebywayofdeath.net	$9.99*/yr SALE!	Save $3.00/yr
☐ hooraykellydonahueisgonebywayofdeath.org	$9.99* SALE!	Save $5.00/yr
☐ hooraykellydonahueisgonebywayofdeath.me	$8.99 SALE!	Save $11.00/yr
☐ hooraykellydonahueisgonebywayofdeath.mobi	$7.99*	Save $7.00/yr
☐ hooraykellydonahueisgonebywayofdeath.us	$9.99/yr SALE!	SPECIAL!
☐ hooraykellydonahueisgonebywayofdeath.biz	$14.99*/yr	

We also recommend...

Why register multiple domains?

Additional	Premium	International

Select All

☐ hooraykellydonahueisgonebywayof...com
☐ thehooraykellydonahueisgonebywa...com
☐ hooraykellydonahueisgonebywayof...com
☐ myhooraykellydonahueisgonebyway...com
☐ hooraykellydonahueisgonebywayof...com
☐ newhooraykellydonahueisgonebyw...com
☐ hooraykellydonahueisgonebywayof...com

HOW HAVE THESE NOT BEEN TAKEN YET ???

LOOKS LIKE KELLY DONAHUE DROPPED A FEW POUNDS. HERE ARE SOME POSSIBLE EXPLANATIONS, ACCOMPANIED BY THE LAS VEGAS ODDS OF THEIR LIKELIHOOD:

HOW KELLY DONAHUE LOST WEIGHT	ODDS
SUPERMARKET STARTED KEEPING THE COOL RANCH DORITOS ON THE TOP SHELF, OUT OF REACH OF HER IMMOBILE SLOTH-ARMS.	2:1
SHE STOPPED USING HER SECOND COW-STOMACH.	3:1
DEEP FRYER BROKE, SO SHE'S HAD TO START EATING HER TWINKIES "HEALTHY-STYLE".	8:1
A 106-YEAR OLD GYPSY CURSED HER FOR RUNNING OVER HIS GYPSY DAUGHTER.	12:1
EVERY OTHER PERSON ON THE PLANET GOT FIVE POUNDS FATTER.	35:1
SHE'S A MYTHICAL SHAPESHIFTER, BUT INSTEAD OF USING HER SUPERNATURAL POWERS TO TRANSFORM INTO SOMETHING BADASS LIKE AN EAGLE OR WATERFALL, SHE CHOSE TO SIMPLY SHAVE A COUPLE POUNDS OFF HER EXISTING LUMPY, DUMPY BODY.	200:1
SHE HIT THE GYM.	1,000,000,000,000,000:1

MISSED MY SUBWAY STOP TODAY BECAUSE
I WAS SO BUSY THINKING ABOUT WAYS
TO ELIMINATE KELLY DONAHUE. IF THIS
WAS THE AMOUNT THAT I WANTED TO
PUNISH HER <u>BEFORE</u> I MISSED MY STOP;

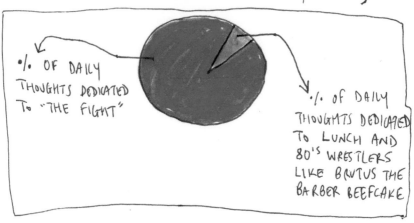

% OF DAILY THOUGHTS DEDICATED TO "THE FIGHT"

% OF DAILY THOUGHTS DEDICATED TO LUNCH AND 80'S WRESTLERS LIKE BRUTUS THE BARBER BEEFCAKE

THIS IS THE REVISED AMOUNT THAT I WANT TO
PUNISH HER <u>AFTER</u> I MISSED MY STOP:

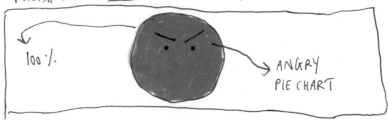

100 %

ANGRY PIE CHART

| 3 | 8 | 11 |

FOUND THIS ON KELLY DONAHUE'S DESK

WHICH MEANS A) SHE IS A GERMAPHOBE
OR B) SHE IS ONTO MY
GERM WARFARE PLOT.

3/10/11

AMAZING DISCOVERY!

So I WAS STARING AT MY ENEMY'S NAME, AS
I DO FOR THE FIRST 20 MINUTES OF
EVERY MORNING, AND I WAS LOOKING FOR
ANY SECRETS HIDDEN INSIDE IT. AND THEN
IT HIT ME:

KELLY DONAHUE UNSCRAMBLES INTO

LE LEAKY HOUND WHICH APPEARS TO BE

FRENCH FOR "THE CRYING DOG". NOW, I
MAY NOT BE A FRENCH EXPERT, BUT I SURE
AS HELL KNOW A SIGN WHEN I SEE ONE.
AND THIS SIGN TELLS ME THINGS WILL
NOT TURN OUT WELL FOR KELLY DONAHUE.

3/11/11

HAD TO MOVE THE CLOCK FORWARD
TODAY FOR DAYLIGHT SAVINGS TIME.
LOST AN HOUR OF STRATEGIZING FOR
"THE FIGHT". WHAT I LOST IN TIME,
I GAINED IN ANGER. 60 MINUTES OF ANGER.
STARTING............ NOW!

3/15/11

BACKSTORY:

I WAS STUCK AT WORK TIL 1AM LAST NIGHT
WITH KELLY DONAHUE. SHE FORGOT HER SUBWAY
PASS AT HOME SO I LENT HER MINE. I FIGURE
$2.25 IS A PRETTY GOOD PRICE TO PAY FOR
THE CHANCE THAT KELLY DONAHUE WILL GET
BRUTALLY MUGGED ON THE F-TRAIN.

COULDN'T FOCUS ON WORK TODAY SO DECIDED TO SPEND ALL DAY RESEARCHING CLASSIC FIGHTS. THEY ALL <u>HAD</u> <u>BADASS</u> <u>NAMES</u>!

THEY HAD STUFF LIKE "THE RUMBLE IN THE JUNGLE" AND "ST. VALENTINE'S DAY MASSACRE" AND "WORLD WAR 2".

SO HERE'S A LIST OF POTENTIAL BADASS NAMES THAT'LL HELP "THE FIGHT" SECURE ITS PLACE IN HISTORY FOREVER.

- "THE LUNCHTIME PUNCHTIME"

- "THE TUESDAY OR WEDNESDAY OR POTENTIALLY FRIDAY BATTLE"

- "THE UNCIVIL WAR"

- "THE KELLY DONAHUE IS GONE HAPPY DANCE DAY"

- "D-DAY" (KELLY DONAHUE'S DEATH-DAY WILL MERIT REASSIGNING "D-DAY" IN HER HONOR.)

3/20/11

① MAKE TO-DO LIST

② MAKE THE WORLD A BETTER
PLACE BY FIGHTING
KELLY DONAHUE TO THE DEATH

ONE DOWN.
ONE TO GO.

3/24/11

TODAY WAS A WEIRD DAY.

KELLY DONAHUE WAS OUT OF THE OFFICE CAUSE
SHE WAS SICK (PROBABLY SICK OF BEING KELLY DONAHUE)
SO I DIDN'T GET TO SEE "THAT FACE"
OR HEAR "THAT VOICE" THAT NORMALLY
GETS ME SUPER AGITATED AND IN A
FIGHTING-TO-THE-DEATH MOOD.

SO... TO KEEP MY MOTIVATION STRONG
AND TO CONSTANTLY REMIND ME OF
JUST HOW MUCH BETTER WE WILL ALL BE
ONCE SHE IS NO LONGER AMONGST US,
HERE IS AN ACCURATE DRAWING THAT CAPTURES
HER IN ALL HER EVILNESS-NESS.

3/26/11

I WAS AT THE GYM TODAY DOING SOME CARDIO AND FREE WEIGHTS (LOW WEIGHT, HIGH REPS) TO BUILD UP STAMINA FOR THE DEATH FIGHT TO END ALL DEATH FIGHTS, AND MY MIND STARTED PONDERING ABOUT THE EXISTENCE OF AN AFTERLIFE.

NOT SURE IF THERE IS A HEAVEN OR HELL BUT IF THERE IS, I'M PRETTY SURE KELLY DONAHUE IS GOING STRAIGHT TO HEAVEN BECAUSE SHE'S THE DEVIL AND THE DEVIL WOULD PROBABLY HATE BEING IN A PLACE FULL OF PURITY AND NOT-ANNOYING PEOPLE.

OH, ON THAT NOTE, I'VE ALSO DECIDED THAT RIGHT BEFORE KELLY DONAHUE'S FACE MAKES CONTACT WITH MY FATAL DEATH ATTACK, I WILL PLAY CHUMBAWUMBA'S "TUBTHUMPING" SO THAT ANNOYING SONG WILL BE STUCK IN HER HEAD IN THE AFTERLIFE. FOREVER!

3/30/11

I HAVE A COLD.
COUGHED ON KELLY DONAHUE'S PHONE.
(SMALL VICTORY.)

4 / 1 / 11

TODAY'S APRIL FOOLS DAY.

DECIDED NOT TO PUT KELLY DONAHUE TO DEATH
TODAY WITH MY DEATH ATTACK.

(JOKE'S ON HER. IT'S STILL ON ITS WAY.)

☆ (REALIZED I'VE BEEN USING (WAY) TOO MANY PARENTHESES.)

☆ AND FOOTNOTE STARS.

4/5/11

I FOLLOWED KELLY DONAHUE HOME FROM WORK.

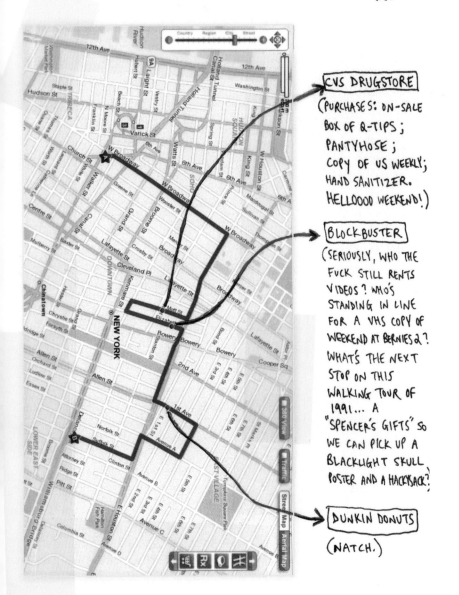

CVS DRUGSTORE

(PURCHASES: ON-SALE
BOX OF Q-TIPS;
PANTYHOSE;
COPY OF US WEEKLY;
HAND SANITIZER.
HELLOOOD WEEKEND!)

BLOCKBUSTER

(SERIOUSLY, WHO THE
FUCK STILL RENTS
VIDEOS? WHO'S
STANDING IN LINE
FOR A VHS COPY OF
WEEKEND AT BERNIE'S 2?
WHAT'S THE NEXT
STOP ON THIS
WALKING TOUR OF
1991... A
"SPENCER'S GIFTS" SO
WE CAN PICK UP A
BLACKLIGHT SKULL
POSTER AND A HACKYSACK?)

DUNKIN DONUTS

(NATCH.)

4/8/11

Across

1 Second Mrs. Trump
6 Venus habitat
12 Tropical fruit
17 Western martial art
18 Used a bat
19 Donkey _____
24 Answer: I
24 Provoke yawns
25 Dieter
26 Foursome
27 Honest Abe
28 Precious metals
29 Carpenter's
   bag of tricks
30 Andrew Lloyd Webber fan club
32 Mechanical bull
34 Latin: tangy
35 Doctor Who start
36 Celestial seasoning
37 Amanda Faye surname
38 Killer bees
40 Foxhounds
43 Author:
   Emily Beth
44 Celestial seasoning
48 Amanda Faye surname

49 The Dow Jones
50 She bites
51 Water to a beggar
53 The cat's meow
55 Hamilton and Rosen
57 Brooklyn native
61 Soon: prefix
62 Potions
64 Poison dart frog
66 Dances a jig
67 Redneck relative
72 Made of copper
73 Answer: II
74 The opposite of the facts
75 Fourth moon mission
76 Epilogue
78 Like apples to oranges
80 Aristotle
81 To fly
83 Your boss doesn't know
85 Mathew or Zachary
87 Fishes for compliments
89 Born again
90 Trouser snake
93 1...2...3...
96 Horse god

98 Sicilian
   port town
99 Clandestino
100 He-Man villain
103 Dancer Radmanovich
104 Conquest (figuratively)
105 To baste
106 Fidgety
107 Orange-red
109 Dr Pepper competitor
111 Scandinavia's 8th president
113 Monsters
115 Answer: III
116 Straight to DVD
120 Eminem alter ego
121 Warned to be on guard
122 Hair accessory
123 Knock knock joke
124 Beezebub nemesis
125 The sound of a sneeze

Down

1 To judge
2 Hentai
3 Carpet inventor
4 Grandiose
5 To overextend one's elbow

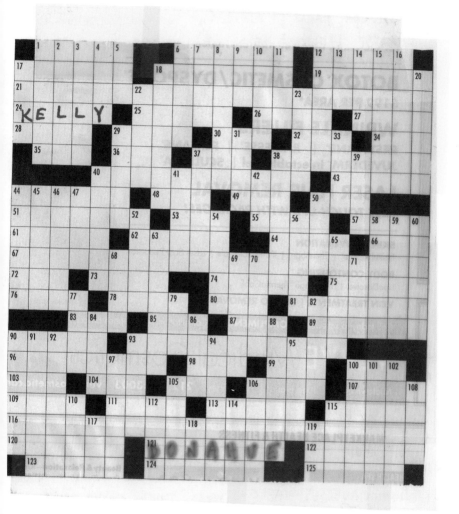

HMMM... BORING & GONNA BE ATTACKED TO DEATH.
WHO COULD IT BE?

UP ALL NIGHT DRINKING COCOA AND WATCHING A CABLE
SPECIAL ON PARALLEL UNIVERSES AND HOW THERE
COULD BE INFINITE OTHER WORLDS OUT THERE THAT

ARE ALMOST EXACTLY
IDENTICAL TO OURS
EXCEPT FOR A TINY
LITTLE THING, LIKE
MAYBE ZEBRAS HAVE
POLKA DOTS, OR THE
FIRST LETTER IN THE
ALPHABET IS 'G'.
OR THERE COULD BE
BIZZARO OPPOSITE
UNIVERSES WHERE
OWLS SAY "TOOH!"
AND FAT PEOPLE
DON'T GRUNT WHEN
THEY WALK UP STAIRS.

Fig. A: *Parallel universe where Kelly Donahue was never born.*

OR THERE COULD BE SOME COMPLETELY WHACKED OUT
RANDOM UNIVERSES WHERE, I DUNNO, THINGS SMELL LIKE
DOORKNOBS. FUCK, I DON'T EVEN KNOW WHAT DOORKNOBS
ARE SUPPOSED TO SMELL LIKE BUT IT'D BE SUPER
UNCOMFORTABLE IF EVERYTHING SMELLED LIKE EM. →

→ AND THEN I STARTED THINKING... FUCK! WHAT IF THERE ARE OTHER PARALLEL UNIVERSES OUT THERE WHERE KELLY DONAHUE IS DIFFERENT? LIKE WHAT IF THERE WAS A WORLD THAT HAD AN OFFICIAL "KELLY DONAHUE HUNTING SEASON"? OR WHAT IF THERE WAS A UNIVERSE WHERE SHE WAS ELECTED PRESIDENT (HA!) AND I WOULD HAFTA GET PAST INSANE SECURITY TO GET TO HER? OR WHAT IF IT WAS WORST CASE SCENARIO AND EVERYONE ON

Fig. B. *Parallel universe where Kelly Donahue is respected.*

THE PLANET WAS KELLY DONAHUE (I JUST BARFED IN MY MOUTH), AS IF THEY'VE ALL BEEN ATTACKED BY SOME GLOBAL BOREDOM VIRUS? DO I DESTROY THEM ALL? DO I TRY TO FIND A CURE? IT'S STUFF LIKE THIS THAT MAKES ME GLAD I'M NOT A SCIENCE GUY AND I ONLY GOTTA DESTROY ONE KELLY DONAHUE TO FEEL COMPLETE.

4/14/11

FEELING CREATIVE. WROTE A HAIKU TO ENGRAVE
IN KELLY DONAHUE'S TOMBSTONE (ASSUMING MY
DEATH ATTACK LEAVES HER BODILY REMAINS IN A
LARGE ENOUGH CHUNK TO BURY.)

KELLY DONAHUE
WILL NO LONGER BOTHER US.
SOMEONE PASS THE CHIPS.

I'M DOING IT!

TIRED OF WAITING AND PLOTTING AND THINKING ABOUT THIS DAMN FIGHT SO I'M GONNA GET IT OVER WITH FOR ONCE AND FOR ALL.

WHEN: TOMORROW, 4:15 PM*

WHERE: WORK

WHAT: FIGHT TO THE DEATH WITH KELLY DONAHUE

HOW: SLOWLY & PAINFULLY

* TO BE FOLLOWED BY CELEBRATORY DRINKS AT TRIBECA TAVERN.

4/27/11

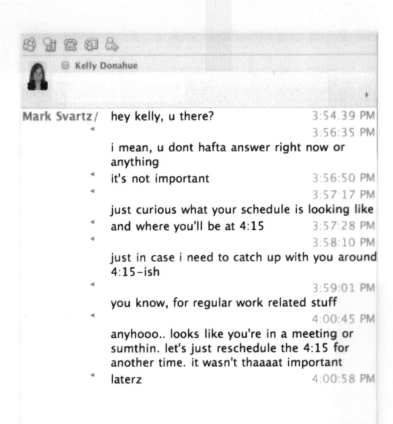

Kelly Donahue

Mark Svartz / hey kelly, u there?   3:54.39 PM

3:56:35 PM
i mean, u dont hafta answer right now or anything

it's not important   3:56:50 PM

3:57:17 PM
just curious what your schedule is looking like
and where you'll be at 4:15   3:57:28 PM

3:58:10 PM
just in case i need to catch up with you around
4:15-ish

3:59:01 PM
you know, for regular work related stuff

4:00:45 PM
anyhooo.. looks like you're in a meeting or
sumthin. let's just reschedule the 4:15 for
another time. it wasn't thaaaat important
laterz   4:00:58 PM

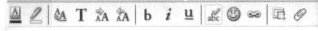

YOU WIN THIS ROUND, KELLY DONAHUE.

5/2/11

IT APPEARS I'VE UNDERESTIMATED YOU, KELLY DONAHUE.
YOU'RE MORE CUNNING THAN YOU LOOK (THEN AGAIN,
WET SOFAS ARE MORE CUNNING THAN YOU LOOK.)

WHICH MEANS, I'M GONNA HAFTA TURN THIS
UP A NOTCH AND START INITIATING SOME
HIGH-LEVEL MENTAL WARFARE. LITTLE BY
LITTLE, I WILL MESS WITH YOUR MIND AND
PUMMEL YOUR BRAIN UNTIL YOU ARE NOTHING
MORE THAN A SHELL OF YOUR BORING SELF.

YOU'VE BROUGHT THIS UPON YOURSELF.

5/3/11

MENTAL ATTACK #1

"HI, I'M KELLY DONAHUE AND I LIKE TO STAPLE
STUFF BECAUSE I'M ANAL LIKE THAT. OH NO!
MY STAPLER WON'T STAPLE! AND IT'S
MAKING A WEIRD CRUNCHY SOUND! WHY
IS IT DOING THAT? WAIT A MINUTE,
ARE THESE CORNFLAKES IN MY STAPLER?
WHO DID THIS? I'M GOING CRAAAZY!"

5/8/11

STARTING TO REALIZE THAT IF THIS
JOURNAL EVER GETS INTO THE WRONG HANDS,
(PARTICULARLY KELLY DONAHUE'S LARGISH MAN-PAWS),
"THE FIGHT" MIGHT GET DERAILED.
SOOOO... FROM NOW ON I WILL BE SPRINKLING
IN PARTICULARLY HIGH-SECURITY MESSAGES
BY MEANS OF AN INDECIPHERABLE CODE:

YLLEK EUHANOD SLLEMS EKIL OOP.

5/14/11

Mark,
Sarah said you were
the one who left the
red velvet cupcake on
my desk.
That was so sweet!
Thanks so much.
☺ Kelly

DID YOU KNOW THAT OBESITY IS QUICKLY BECOMING THE #1 KILLER IN THE U.S.? THERE'S MORE CUPCAKES WHERE THAT CAME FROM, KELLY DONAHUE.

5/17/11

IN PREPARATION FOR "THE FIGHT", I'VE BEEN
REFLECTING ON PAST BATTLES THAT I FOUGHT
OVER THE YEARS. LOOKING BACK, THE ONE ENEMY
THAT I HAD THE MOST SATISFACTION DEFEATING
WAS "GREAT TIGER", THE MUMBAI MYSTIC
BOXER FROM MIKE TYSON'S "PUNCH-OUT".

IT TOOK ME THREE MONTHS TO FIGURE OUT HOW
TO CONQUER GREAT TIGER. AND SOON I WILL
APPLY THE EXACT MOVES I USED AGAINST HIM
TO TAKE ON KELLY DONAHUE IN OUR UPCOMING
DEATH BRAWL.

~~KELLY DONAHUE~~
[~~GREAT TIGER~~] PUNCH SEQUENCE

1. AT THE BEGINNING OF THE FIGHT ~~HE~~ SHE WILL THROW A PUNCH. DODGE IT AND HIT ~~HIM~~ HER IN THE FACE.

2. PUNCH (~~HE~~ SHE BLOCKS IT.)

3. DODGE.

4. PUNCH (CONNECT.)

5. PUNCH (~~HE~~ SHE BLOCKS IT.)

6. DODGE.

7. PUNCH (CONNECT.)

8. PUNCH (~~HE~~ SHE BLOCKS IT.)

9. DODGE.

10. PUNCH (CONNECT.)

11. ~~HE~~ SHE WILL ATTEMPT AN UPPERCUT. DODGE IT AND HIT ~~HIM~~ HER IN THE FACE 4-6X.

12. THROW BODY BLOWS AS ~~HE~~ SHE BEGINS MOTION OF ~~HIS~~ HER UPPERCUT.

13. ~~HE~~ SHE BACKS UP AND STARTS SPINNING AROUND THE RING LIKE A MADMAN. EACH TIME ~~HE~~ SHE GOES AROUND ~~HE~~ SHE WILL THROW A PUNCH. BLOCK IT EACH TIME ~~HE~~ SHE GOES AROUND BY DUCKING DOWN. THIS MUST BE TIMED RIGHT.

14. AFTER 5X GOING AROUND, ~~HE~~ SHE WILL BE ALL DIZZY AND JUST STAND THERE. SMACK ~~HIM~~ HER IN THE FACE TO KNOCK ~~HIM~~ HER OUT.

5/21/11

Recently Viewed Items

Real Bodybag U.S. Government issue

$50.00

- Watch this item
- View seller's other items
- View similar items

Time Left: 24d 9h 26m

Round Nose Garden Shovel with Fiberglass D-Handle

$12.95

- Watch this item
- View seller's other items
- View similar items

Time Left: 14d 22h 16m

CONGRATS Round Shape Mylar Balloon 18"

$3.50

- Watch this item
- View seller's other items
- View similar items

Time Left: 14d 8h 11m

Clear all

HARD TO RESIST A GOOD BARGAIN.

I'VE GOTTA START GETTING SERIOUS ABOUT THIS STUFF. NO MORE PROCRASTINATING. I'VE GOTTA JUST SET A GOAL DATE, KINDA LIKE THOSE CHUBBY WEIGHTWATCHERS PEOPLE DO. EXCEPT INSTEAD OF TRYING TO DROP 15 POUNDS OF FAT, I'm TRYING TO DROP 130 POUNDS OF BORING. *

---

* I ALSO HEREBY PROPOSE THAT THE INTERNATIONAL SYSTEM OF UNITS ADOPT THE TERM "KELLY DONAHUE" AS AN OFFICIAL UNIT OF MEASUREMENT. MUCH AS THE KELVIN (K) MEASURES TEMPERATURE AND THE WATT (W) MEASURES ENERGY, THE KELLY DONAHUE (KD) SHOULD MEASURE BOREDOM.
EXAMPLE: NASCAR IS 4 KDs MORE BORING THAN SOCCER.

5/26/11

SO, IN OTHER NEWS...

WHAT. THE.

FUCK!

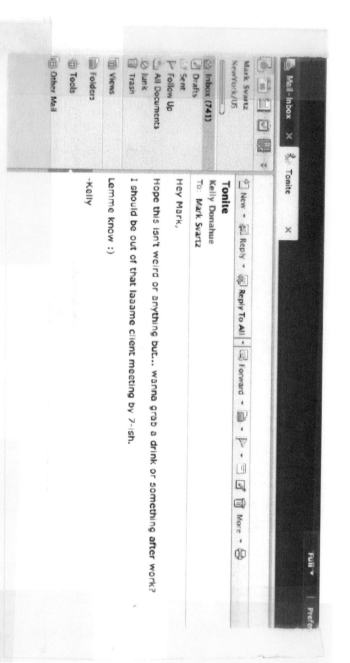

Mail - Inbox × | 🐿 Tonite ×

Mark Svartz
NewYork/US

Inbox (741)
Drafts
Sent
Follow Up
All Documents
Junk
Trash
Views
Folders
Tools
Other Mail

New ▾ | Reply ▾ | Reply To All | ▾ | Forward ▾ | ▾ | ▾ | ▾ | More ▾ |

Tonite

Kelly Donahue
To: Mark Svartz

Hey Mark,

Hope this isn't weird or anything but... wanna grab a drink or something after work?

I should be out of that laaame client meeting by 7-ish.

Lemme know :)

-Kelly

Full ▾ | Prefe

UGH!. SO THIS CAN GO ONE OF TWO WAYS:

IF I SAY **NO**, HER FEELINGS WILL GET HURT AND THAT'S ALMOST AS FULFILLING AS HER BODY BEING HURT, SO... PRETTY AWESOME. <u>BUT</u>, THEN I OPENLY BECOME HER ENEMY AND HER DEFENSES WILL BE UP, MAKING IT MORE DIFFICULT TO TRY TO DECAPITATE HER AND STUFF LIKE THAT.

SHORT TERM: HIGH FIVE!

LONG TERM: BUMMER.

IF I SAY **YES**, I WILL HAVE TO ENDURE SOME OF THE MOST SKIN-CRAWLING, STOMACH-TURNING, TORTUOUS FEAR-FACTOR CONDITIONS IMAGINABLE. <u>BUT</u>, THIS WILL GIVE ME UNLIMITED ACCESS TO KELLY DONAHUE, 24/7, MAKING HER COMPLETELY VULNERABLE TO THE SURPRISE DEATH ATTACK OF MY CHOICE.

SHORT TERM: I JUST PUKED IN MY MOUTH.

LONG TERM: VICTORY.

YOU LEAVE ME NO CHOICE. I WILL DATE YOU KELLY DONAHUE. AND YOU WILL REGRET EVERY ROMANTIC SECOND OF IT.

MANAGED TO POSTPONE "THE DATE" FOR A FEW
DAYS. THIS GAVE ME A LITTLE TIME TO THINK
THINGS OUT AND PLAN THE CONVERSATION
FOR OPTIMUM DATA GATHERING. HERE'S WHAT
I'VE COME UP WITH SO FAR:

THINGS TO TALK ABOUT:

- HER FAVORITE HIDING SPOTS.
- THE ABSURDITY OF LOCKING DOORS.
- WHERE SHE LIKES TO HANG OUT ON
  NIGHTS THAT SHE'S BY HERSELF.
- THE MOVIE "THE NOTEBOOK". (JUST TO
  THROW HER OFF.)
- FOODS/THINGS SHE'S ALLERGIC TO, AND
  JUST HOW ALLERGIC.

THINGS NOT TO TALK ABOUT:

- KILLING HER.

Local business results for **good date place for someone i hate** near New York, NY

(A) NY Penta Hotel
www.hotelpenn.com - (212) 290-2224 - 2351 reviews

(B) Phillips Electronics North America Corporation
maps.google.com - (800) 223-1828 - 1160 reviews

(C) Belvedere Hotel
belvederehotelnyc.com - (212) 245-7000 - 1700 reviews

(D) Le Souk Inc
www.lesoukny.com - (212) 777-5454 - 328 reviews

(E) Otto Restaurant Enoteca Pizza
www.ottopizzeria.com - (212) 995-9559 - 336 reviews

(F) Hudson Hotel
www.hudsonhotel.com - (212) 554-6000 - 2266 reviews

(G) Algonquin Hotel
www.algonquinhotel.com - (212) 840-6800 - 725 reviews

More results near New York, NY »

ALRIGHT. IT'S REALLY FUCKING HAPPENING TONIGHT. IF I CLEAR MY MIND AND GO TO MY HAPPY-PLACE AND TREAT THIS "DATE" AS PURELY A RECONAISSANCE MISSION LIKE AN ARMY RANGER HAVING TO CRAWL THROUGH A SHIT CREEK TO GET BEHIND ENEMY LINES, I'LL BE A-OK. BUT, IF THINGS GO HORRIBLY WRONG AND I DON'T RETURN AND SOMEONE IS TO DISCOVER THIS JOURNAL, IT MEANS ONE OF TWO THINGS:

① I LITERALLY DIED OF BOREDOM TONIGHT.

—————— OR ——————

② SHE WAS SO ANNOYING THAT I JUST WENT AHEAD AND ENDED "THE FIGHT" AND I AM NOW ON THE RUN FROM THE LAW, PROBABLY LIVING UNDER A NEW IDENTITY AS A BOAT BUILDER ON SOME WHITE SANDY MEXICAN BEACH WITH AN OLD FRIEND FROM PRISON (WAIT, I'M THINKING OF THE ENDING FROM SHAWSHANK REDEMPTION. FUCK THAT MOVIE WAS GOOD!)

WELL EITHER WAY, IF I'M NOT AROUND, IT'S UP TO YOU TO PASS THIS STORY ON. FUTURE GENERATIONS MUST BE TOLD OF THE HORRORS OF THIS CREATURE KNOWN AS KELLY DONAHUE.

"AB UNO DISCE OMNES". ⟶ (THAT'S LATIN, BITCHES!)

(8:42 PM)→ GOT HERE EARLY SO I COULD
SCOPE OUT THE EMERGENCY EXITS.
THIS BETTER BE WORTH IT.

(9:29 PM)→ SHE'S IN THE BATHROOM. SO FAR,
SPENT 48 MINUTES TALKING ABOUT WORK
AND THE REST WAS ME NODDING ALONG
WHILE TRYING TO NOT JAB HER
JUGULAR WITH A FORK. I RECALL
RANDOM BITS ABOUT CO-ED SOFTBALL,
LABRADOODLES (?), AND A TRIP TO
NAPA WITH "THE GIRLS". $50 SAYS
THOSE GEMS WERE PULLED STRAIGHT
FROM HER MATCH.com PROFILE.
I HATE HER SO MUCH!

(10:37 PM)→ ON A SUBWAY HOME.
DIDN'T KISS HER. DIDN'T KILL HER.
I GUESS IT GOES ON. TIL DEATH DO US PART.

6/8/11

SOME GUY AT WORK ASKED ME HOW MY DATE
WITH KELLY DONAHUE WENT LAST NIGHT, AND
IT KINDA FELT LIKE SOMEONE ASKING ME
HOW MY TESTICULAR CANCER WAS DOING.
IT'S A PRETTY ROUGH THING TO COPE WITH, SO
I MADE THE FOLLOWING LIST TO CHEER ME UP:

THINGS THAT ARE WAY WORSE THAN DATING KELLY DONAHUE

- HAVING THE TIP OF YOUR TONGUE CUT OFF AND
THEN SUCKING ON A LEMON DROP WHILE WATCHING
"THE USUAL SUSPECTS" FOR THE FIRST TIME AND JUST
BEFORE THE CLIMACTIC REVEAL, SOMEONE ACCIDENTALLY
TELLS YOU THAT KEVIN SPACEY WAS KAISER SOZE.

- BLACK LICORICE

- AIDS (BUT ONLY THE REALLY BAD KIND. NOT THE KIND
THAT STILL LETS YOU PLAY BASKETBALL
AND OPEN MOVIE THEATERS.)

~~Waterboarding~~ DATING KELLY DONAHUE

From Wikipedia, the free encyclopedia

For the aquatic sport sometimes known as "water boarding", see Surfing.

~~Waterboarding~~ DATING KELLY DONAHUE is a form of torture that consists of immobilizing the subject ~~on his back~~ IN A RESTAURANT with the head inclined downwards; ~~water~~ BOREDOM is then poured over the face into ~~breathing~~ LISTENING passages, causing the captive to experience the sensations of ~~drowning~~ YAWNING.[1][2] In contrast to submerging the head face-forward in water, ~~waterboarding~~ DATING KELLY DONAHUE precipitates an almost immediate gag reflex.[3] It can cause extreme pain, dry ~~drowning~~ HEANING, damage to ~~lungs~~ REPUTATION, brain damage from ~~oxygen~~ INTERESTING CONVERSATION deprivation, other physical injuries including broken bones due to struggling against restraints, lasting psychological damage or, if uninterrupted, death.[4] Adverse physical consequences can manifest themselves months after the event, while psychological effects can last for years.[5]

The term ~~waterboarding~~ DATING KELLY DONAHUE was coined in ~~2004~~ 2009.[6][7]

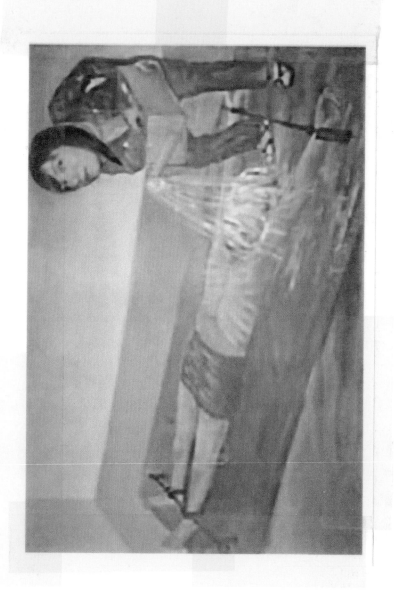

6/18/11

WENT ON A COUPLE MORE DATES. YES, WE KISSED. AND
THERE'S NO SUGARCOATING THIS ONE.

IT WAS AWFUL.

IT KINDA REMINDED ME OF THE FIRST TIME
I ATE BRUSSEL SPROUTS AS A KID, AND I
PINCHED MY NOSE SHUT WHEN I CHEWED SO
I DIDN'T HAFTA TASTE THE EVIL. WELL,
THIS TIME I COULDN'T PINCH MY NOSE.
I SMELLED IT ALL. IT REEKED OF
CORNED BEEF AND SHAME.

That's where the monster touched me, doctor!

7/4/11

WE SURVIVED THE BRITISH.[1]
WE SURVIVED THE NAZIS.[2]
WE SURVIVED THE COMMIES.[3]
YES, WE WILL SURVIVE YOU TOO, KELLY DONAHUE.[4]

HAPPY INDEPENDENCE DAY!

---

[1] "THE AMERICAN REVOLUTION"

[2] "WORLD WAR TWO"

[3] "THE COLD WAR"

[4] "THE FIGHT"

7/6/11

SO IT'S BEEN A MONTH TO THE DAY THAT I
STEPPED ACROSS ENEMY LINES TO "DATE"
THE BEAST. WHICH MEANS THAT UNLESS SHE
BUYS MY "I'M SAVING MYSELF FOR MARRIAGE"
EXCUSE... I'M GONNA HAFTA PUT IT IN HER.
NOW NORMALLY THIS WOULD BE THE POINT
WHEN A SOLDIER WAVES HIS WHITE FLAG,
A BOXER'S CORNERMAN THROWS IN THE TOWEL,
AN ULTIMATE FIGHTER TAPS OUT. BUT I DID
NOT COME THIS FAR TO RUN AWAY WITH
MY TAIL BETWEEN MY LEGS WHEN THE
GOING GOT ROUGH. NOT ONLY WILL I NOT
BACK AWAY, BUT I WILL CONTINUE TO
FORGE AHEAD; CHIN UP, CHEST OUT, PANTS DOWN,
AS I PLANT ANOTHER GRENADE INTO KELLY
DONAHUE'S DEEP COBWEBBED BUNKER.

❝ OPPORTUNITIES MULTIPLY
   AS THEY ARE SEIZED ❞
        — SUN TZU, THE ART OF WAR

 (SAD PENISES)

I'VE ALWAYS LOVED THE PREMISE OF PIXAR'S "MONSTERS INC.", WHERE AT FIRST THEY WENT ABOUT MINING ENERGY FROM THE POWER OF CHILDREN'S SCREAMS, BUT EVENTUALLY THEY DISCOVERED THAT THEY COULD ACTUALLY GET EVEN MORE POWER OUT OF CHILDREN'S LAUGHTER.

WELL, THE OTHER NIGHT I MADE A SIMILAR DISCOVERY. I USED TO THINK THAT IT TOOK THINGS LIKE LUST AND PASSION, PERHAPS EVEN LOVE, TO ENTICE AN ERECTION COBRA OUT OF ITS BASKET. YET AFTER BEING FORCED BY SHE WHO SHALL NOT BE NAMED TO ENGAGE IN SOME CARNAL INTERCOURSE (THOUGH →

→ AFTER WITNESSING SOME OF HER TOOTHY
O-FACES, I SHOULD PROBABLY CALL IT
"INTER-HORSE"), I'VE NOW LEARNED THAT
A LOVE-FUELED BONER IS <u>NOTHING</u>
COMPARED TO ONE POWERED BY PURE
AND UTTER DISGUST.

<u>NOTE</u>: MUST TALK TO SCIENTISTS ABOUT
BOTTLING THIS. IT SHALL BE
CALLED "VIANGER". SIDE EFFECTS
MAY INCLUDE INSOMNIA AND
SELF-HATRED.

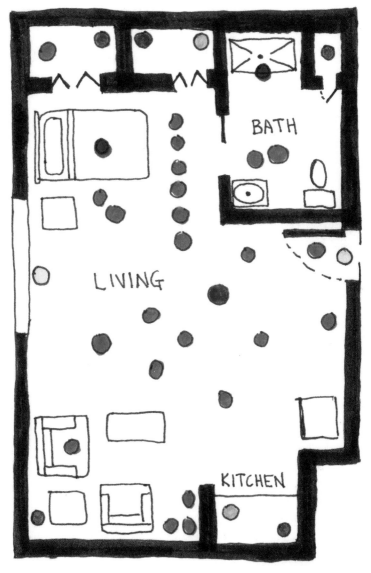

BATH

LIVING

KITCHEN

KELLY DONAHUE'S APARTMENT LAYOUT

KEY

- ● PLACE TO HIDE BODY
- ● PLACE TO HIDE BODY PARTS
- ○ ESCAPE ROUTES
- ● LOCATION OF KNIVES/TOOLS
- ● PLACES I WANNA FIGHT HER
- ● GOOD SPOT FOR AN AREA RUG

7/24/11

Dan Smith Will Teach You Guitar

HOW TO KILL KELLY DONAHUE WITH A

AS SOON AS KELLY DONAHUE'S BODY IS FOUND (AFTER "THE FIGHT") AND THE MANHUNT BEGINS, THESE ALTERED CARDS WILL CONVENIENTLY APPEAR IN EVERY SINGLE BAR, CLUB, AND BODEGA IN NEW YORK CITY. JUST SAYIN', THIS MIGHT BE A GOOD TIME FOR YOU TO CHANGE UP THAT SERIAL KILLER HAIRCUT, DAN.

7/28/11

DISCOVERED THAT KELLY DONAHUE IS REALLY ALLERGIC
TO PEANUTS. ALSO DISCOVERED THAT I REALLY
LOVE TO BAKE.

SUPER-PEANUTTY PEANUT BUTTER NUTTER COOKIES

8 OZ NATURAL UNSALTED PEANUT BUTTER
1/2 CUP CHOPPED UNSALTED PEANUTS
1 EGG
3/4 CUP SUGAR
1/2 TSP BAKING SODA
1/4 TSP KOSHER SALT
6 OZ CHOCOLATE CHUNKS

PREHEAT OVEN TO 350°. MIX PEANUT BUTTER, EGG, SUGAR, BAKING
SODA, AND SALT THOROUGHLY, THEN STIR IN PEANUTS AND
CHOCOLATE CHUNKS. DROP BY SPOONFULS ONTO A PARCHMENT-
LINED COOKIE SHEET AND BAKE FOR 12 MIN, UNTIL GOLDEN
AND PUFFY. WHEN DONE, LET THEM SET FOR A FEW MINUTES
BEFORE REMOVING FROM COOKIE SHEETS.

SERVINGS: MAKES 36 COOKIES, BUT SHOULD DO THE JOB IN ONE.

8/2/11

SO IT'S BEEN 7 MONTHS SINCE I FIRST REALIZED MY
CALLING TO END THE EXISTENCE OF KELLY DONAHUE,
AND I'M GETTING PRETTY EXHAUSTED OF THIS THING
GROWING INSIDE OF ME. I WANT IT OUT!
IT'S KINDA LIKE I'M PREGNANT AND I'VE JUST ENTERED
THE FINAL TRIMESTER. BUT AT 28 WEEKS, MY
DEATH PLAN IS TOO LATE TO ABORT, BUT TOO
UNDERDEVELOPED TO RELEASE UNTO THE WORLD.

PLAN AT 28 WEEKS

PLAN AT FULL TERM

I'M GONNA GIVE THIS BUN A LITTLE MORE TIME IN THE
OVEN TO MATURE AND GROW THOSE NECESSARY BITS
AND PIECES. BUT THE DUE DATE IS QUICKLY
APPROACHING, KELLY DONAHUE. AND THIS BABY'S PISSED.

8/6/11

                                    THREE
A PICTURE SAYS ~~A THOUSAND~~ WORDS: "YOU DISGUST ME".

8/11/11

THIS QUEST THAT I'VE BEEN ON SINCE JANUARY HAS
FORCED ME TO DRILL DEEP INTO THE DEPTHS OF MY
SOUL TO DISCOVER THE HIDDEN TRUTHS THAT
ARE BURIED WITHIN ME.

ONE SOURCE OF SPIRITUAL STRENGTH FOR ME AS
I EMBARK ON THE FINAL LEG OF THIS VOYAGE
IS THE NATIVE AMERICAN BELIEF IN "TOTEM ANIMALS".
IT IS SAID THAT EACH INDIVIDUAL IS CONNECTED
FOR LIFE WITH A DIFFERENT ANIMAL THAT
SERVES AS A PARTNER AND GUIDE THROUGH
LIFE'S MANY JOURNEYS.

EACH TOTEM ANIMAL HAS ITS OWN UNIQUE VALUES
AND ATTRIBUTES. FOR EXAMPLE, THE CROCODILE
REPRESENTS "QUICKNESS & AGGRESSION." THE
BUMBLEBEE REPRESENTS "ORGANIZATION & COMMUNITY."
THE UNICORN REPRESENTS " PURITY, INNOCENCE,
AND GENTLE STRENGTH."   ⟹

→ THAT SAID, I HAVE DISCOVERED THAT
MY VERY OWN TOTEM ANIMAL IS THE PANDA!

IT REPRESENTS "PATIENCE, DETERMINATION, & KARATE."
THE PANDA IS NOT ONE TO MAKE STUPID DECISIONS
LIKE THE JAGUAR, AND IT'S NOT A WEAK
LITTLE BITCH LIKE THE OSTRICH.

NO, THE PANDA IS A QUIET, CALCULATED,
FURRY-ASSED GENIUS AND HE WILL GIVE ME
ALL THE SPIRITUAL STRENGTH AND BAMBOO I
NEED TO FULFILL MY CONQUEST OF HATE.

(P.S.- KELLY DONAHUE'S TOTEM ANIMAL IS THE DODO.)
CAUSE IT'S DEAD.

8/19/11

STILL HATCHING PLAN.
BUT IT SHOULD END
SOMETHING LIKE
THIS ⟶

No one important died today

Kelly Donahue found dead

This isn't exactly "newsworthy" news, but the body of a woman named Kelly Donahue was found on a park bench in Central Park yesterday morning.

At first, police officers were completely mystified by what they saw. As NYPD Detective Miles Greller reports, "We had no freaking clue what that thing was. Officer Harvey thought it was a sack of rotten potatoes, cause of the shape and odor. Lieutenant Corbo thought it was a dead seal with a bad wig. I kinda figured it was a human being, but the

President Obama approves.

gender was questionable. To be honest, I read her driver's license and I still question that gender thing."

Donahue, who was in her late.

20's yet dressed like someone in her early 80's, was found slumped on a bench at 8:46 AM, surrounded by a swarm of pigeons who also didn't seem to really care much about her.

"This kinda thing happens all the time. But usually we care more about them. This time, we were all like 'Whatever. Who wants pancakes?'", said EMT worker Frida Kohen.

In other inconsequential news that nobody cares about: a recyclable glass bottle was discovered in a regular garbage bin in Staten Island; Belle Harbor kids Amanda, Emily and Matty Vaysman wanted macaroni for dinner but they instead got tuna casserole and they still ate it; several old Flatbush ladies lost in bingo.

Synopsis: Aaron Eckhart and Jennifer Aniston star in the romantic drama Love Happens. When a self-help author arrives in Seattle to teach a sold-out seminar, he unexpectedly meets the one person who might finally be able to help him help himself

THE SAD THING → OUT OF ALL THE AMAZING MASTERPIECES IN THE HISTORY OF FILM, THIS JENNIFER ANISTON GEM IS PROBABLY THE LAST MOVIE KELLY DONAHUE WILL EVER GET TO EXPERIENCE.

THE SADDER THING → SHE PROBABLY WOULDN'T MIND.

8/23/11

CRAAAAAAAAAAAAAAAAAAZY IDEA!
WHAT IF I TOOK IT TO THE NEXT LEVEL AND ACTUALLY
MARRIED KELLY DONAHUE??? NOT ONLY COULD I MAKE
HER LIVE IN FEAR FOR LIKE 40 YEARS, BUT HER FAMILY
COULD SUPPLY ALL MY "FIGHT" SUPPLIES!

Wedding Registry

WELCOME, MARK SVARTZ and **KELLY DONAHUE**

August 23, 2011
NEW YORK, NY
Edit Your Registry Information

Review what your guests will see. <u>Review</u>
Print your registry to take it with you. <u>Print</u>

My Registry

Description	Price	Availability	Wants	Has	Remove
<u>SOG SOGFari Machete, 13</u> **SOG SPECIALTY KNIVES**	$17.98	**Online Only**	3	0	☐
<u>Miracle Blade III 11-Piece Knife Set</u> **IDEAL PRODUCTS LLC** ★★★★★	$19.94	**Online Only**	1	0	☐
<u>3.5-Pound Axe</u> **AMES TRUE TEMPER** ★★★★★	$21.00	**Sold Online Sold in Stores**	1	0	☐
<u>Gerber Gator Combo Axe</u> **GERBER** ★★★★★	$34.31	**Online Only**	1	0	☐
<u>Poulan 14" Woodshark Chainsaw</u> **HUSQVARNA OUTDOOR PRODUCTS INC** ★★★★☆	$97.97	**Sold Online Sold in Stores**	1	0	☐

8/27/11

THE CLOSER I GET TO "THE FIGHT", THE MORE
CONSCIOUS I AM OF JUST HOW MASSIVELY THIS
WILL IMPACT LIFE AS WE KNOW IT.

IT'S KINDA SORTA LIKE THE "BUTTERFLY EFFECT",
WHICH IS A METAPHOR COINED BY MATHEMATICIAN
AND METEOROLOGIST EDWARD NORTON LORENZ THAT
ENCAPSULATES THE CONCEPT OF SENSITIVE
DEPENDENCE ON INITIAL CONDITIONS IN CHAOS
THEORY. BUT IN LAYMAN'S TERMS FOR ALL
YOU NON-MATHEMATICIANS AND/OR METEOROLOGISTS,
IT'S A THEORY ABOUT HOW EVEN THE TEENIEST
TINIEST FLAP OF A STUPID LITTLE BUTTERFLY'S
WINGS CAN CAUSE SOME SUPER CRAZY ➔↗

"THE FIGHT'S BUTTERFLY EFFECT OF AWESOMENESS:

 KELLY DONAHUE'S DEATH  EVERYONE CELEBRATES ➔

GIGANTIC NATURAL DISASTER OR METEOR SHOWER ON THE OTHER SIDE OF THE PLANET. SO, EVEN THOUGH KELLY DONAHUE IS AS INSIGNIFICANT AS HUMANLY POSSIBLE, DESTROYING HER MIGHT STILL CAUSE SOME AMAZING CHAIN REACTION OF AWESOMENESS. I MEAN, MAYBE HER DEATH WILL INSPIRE WORLD PEACE. OR END GLOBAL WARMING. OR RESURRECT THE PATHETIC CAREER OF STEVE GUTTENBERG.

I GOTTA ADMIT, IT FEELS GOOD KNOWING THAT ELIMINATING KELLY DONAHUE AND HER VEGGIE BURGER BREATH WILL NOT ONLY MAKE MY LIFE HAPPIER, BUT IT'LL MAKE THE WHOLE WORLD A BETTER PLACE.

 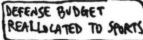

NO MORE WARS → DEFENSE BUDGET REALLOCATED TO SPORTS → METS WIN WORLD SERIES

SOME OF YOU MAY REMEMBER **SEPTEMBER 22** AS THE DAY IN 1236 THAT THE LITHUANIANS AND SEMIGALLIANS DEFEATED THE LIVONIAN BROTHERS OF THE SWORD IN THE BATTLE OF SAULE.

SOME OF YOU MAY FONDLY RECALL **SEPTEMBER 22** AS THE DAY IN 1994 THAT THE NORDHORDLAND BRIDGE WAS OPENED ACROSS THE SALHUSFJORDAN BETWEEN KLAUVANESET AND FLATØY IN HORDALAND, NORWAY.

AND I'M SURE SOME OF YOU COMMEMORATE **SEPTEMBER 22** AS THE BIRTHDAY OF GERMAN PHILOLOGIST PHILLIPP NIKODEMUS FRISHSCHLIN (1547), LITHUANIAN PAINTER MIKALOJUS KONSTANTINAS CIURLIONIS (1875), OR JAPANESE SWIMMER KOSUKE KITAJIMA (1982).

BUT SINCE **SEPTEMBER 22** IS ALSO THE DAY THAT KELLY DONAHUE FINALLY RETURNS FROM HER COUSIN'S WEEKEND BACHELORETTE PARTY IN MIAMI, I HEREBY INVITE YOU TO JOIN ME AS WE ADD "KELLY DONAHUE'S DEATH FIGHT TO THE DEATH" (2011) TO THE LONG LIST OF THINGS TO CELEBRATE ON THIS VERY SPECIAL DAY OF THE YEAR.

Save The Date!!!

SEPTEMBER 22, 2011

There will be reggae music, party games, and the death of Kelly Donahue.

R.S.V.P by September 20th so we know how much spinach dip to make. We look forward to sharing this special occasion with you.

9/3/11

ME: IF YOU HAD TO HAVE A LAST MEAL, WHAT WOULD IT BE?

KELLY DONAHUE: Hmm... PROBABLY MAC & CHEESE WITH TATER TOTS AND A VANILLA SHAKE.

ME: OK.

9/7/11

Cleaner for 1 bdrm apt. - Wed. 9/23

Date: 2011-09-07, 10:35PM EDT
Reply to: serv-vhepb-1737809801@craigslist.org

Looking for experienced house cleaner to sweep up after "party"

Must be able to:
- Remove "fruit punch" stains on carpet and sofa and curtains and walls and windows and doorknobs.
- Deodorize smell of "burnt food"
- Drag away roughly 128 lbs. of "trash"

Fees "negotiable"

Formula for Completing Your Bucket List:

First. Decide what you want.
DEFEAT KELLY DONAHUE IN A FIGHT TO THE DEATH.
Second. Create specific, measurable, time-bound goals.
I WILL STAND OVER HER LIFELESS BODY ON TUES., 9/22.
Third. Know why you want to achieve each goal. JUST BECAUSE.

Fourth. Set an empowering belief.
I BELIEVE KELLY DONAHUE MUST DIE IN A FIGHT TO THE DEATH.
Fifth. Commit focus and attention to your goal. YOU MEAN LIKE NINE MONTHS OF COPIOUS NOTES AND DETAILED DRAWINGS?
Sixth. Take the most obvious actions to achieve your goal.
MY ACTIONS WILL BE PRETTY OBVIOUS.
Seventh. Measure and monitor your progress, adjusting your actions to realign with your goal. SEE JOURNAL.

9/18/11

KELLY DONAHUE TAKES OFF FOR MIAMI TODAY.

ONLY FOUR DAYS TIL I GET MY HANDS ON HER!

(PLEASE NO PLANE CRASH.)
(PLEASE NO PLANE CRASH.)
(PLEASE NO PLANE CRASH.)

YOU'RE WELCOME, BETH ISRAEL MEDICAL CENTER.

9/20/11

THIS IS WHAT I FEEL LIKE INSIDE RIGHT NOW.
(2 DAYS TIL THE FIGHT. YAY!)

9/21/11

HAVEN'T HEARD FROM KELLY DONAHUE ALL DAY.
SHE'S PROBABLY JUST EXHAUSTED FROM TOO MANY
WINE SPRITZERS AND SEX & THE CITY DEBATES...
("YOU'RE SAMANTHA! SHUT UP... YOOOOU'RE SAMANTHA!")

WHATEV, NO BIGGIE. WE DON'T NEED TO CHAT. CAUSE
TOMORROW NIGHT WE'LL HAVE PLENTY TO TALK ABOUT.
WITH OUR FISTS!!!
AND I'M GONNA HAVE THE LAST WORD.
ALSO WITH MY FISTS!!!

9/22/11

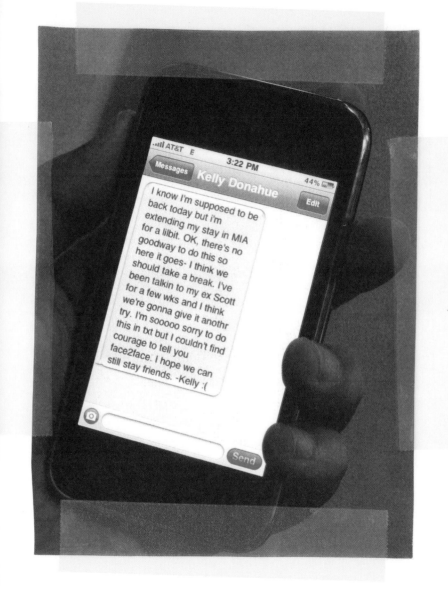

DEAR KELLY DONAHUE,

FIRST OF ALL, STOP ENDING TEXTS AND EMAILS WITH SMILEY/FROWNY FACES. IF I CAN'T GAUGE YOUR EMOTIONAL STATUS AFTER READING AN ENTIRE EMAIL, ALL AN EMOTICON WILL CLARIFY IS THAT YOU'RE OFFICIALLY RETARDED.

SECOND OF ALL, GO FUCK YOURSELF :)

HONESTLY, I DON'T GIVE A RAT'S ASS THAT YOU'RE BREAKING UP WITH ME. AND I DON'T CARE THAT YOU'RE DOING IT IN THE LAMEST, MOST CHICKENSHIT WAY POSSIBLE. BUT WHAT I **DO** CARE ABOUT IS THAT THIS ONE IDIOTIC MOVE OF YOURS HAS SINGLEHANDEDLY DESTROYED ALL OF MY CAREFUL PLANNING FOR "THE FIGHT", AND FOR THAT I WILL NEVER FORGIVE YOU.

I MEAN, HOW CAN I KILL YOU NOW? THE WHOLE POINT OF THE FIGHT WAS THAT IT WOULD BE THE GREATEST, MOST EPIC BATTLE THE WORLD HAS EVER SEEN. IT WOULD'VE GONE DOWN IN HISTORY BOOKS. IT WOULD'VE BEEN THE STUFF OF LEGENDS AND FOLKLORES. IT WOULD'VE BEEN THE INSPIRATION FOR AN OSCAR-NOMINATED FILM DIRECTED BY RON HOWARD AND FEATURING HIS MENTALLY-CHALLENGED BROTHER CLINT IN A CAMEO ROLE.

BUT NOW? NOW YOUR MURDER IS JUST SO FUCKING EXPECTED. KILLING YOU WOULD AT BEST COME ACROSS AS SOME REGULAR OL' CASE OF A JILTED BOYFRIEND'S JEALOUS RAGE. WHO'S GONNA BELIEVE THAT "THE FIGHT" HAD NOTHING TO DO WITH GETTING DUMPED? WHO'S GONNA BELIEVE THAT I PUT **9 MONTHS** OF PAINSTAKING EFFORT INTO THIS BATTLE? WHO'S GONNA BELIEVE THAT I HAD FIVE INTRICATELY DETAILED POTENTIAL DEATH ATTACKS JUST WAITING TO BE EXECUTED???

DEATH PLAN "A": THE ATTACK OF

STAGE THE BATTLE SO IT LOOKS LIKE IT WAS
DONE BY SOME MYSTERIOUS GERMAN GIANT.

① STEREO BLASTING
   SOME HASSELHOFF

② EUROPEAN MEN'S SIZE 49
   FOOTPRINTS
   (THAT'S HUUUGE!)

THE GERMAN GIANT

③ HALF-EATEN PLATE OF GERMAN BRATWURST WITH SAURKRAUT.

④ SIZE XXXXL BLOODY GLOVE IN TRASH.

DEATH PLAN "B": THE STAGED SUICIDE THAT WAS

WITH HELP FROM HER VERY OWN CAT, MAKE PEOPLE
THINK KELLY DONAHUE TOOK HER OWN LAME LIFE.

① NOOSE. (WITH SUPER STRONG KNOT
SHE CAN'T UNTIE WITH
HER MANNISH SAUSAGE
FINGERS.)

② BLOCK OF FROZEN MILK
THAT HER FEET WILL REST ON
UNTIL IT MELTS AWAY.

③ CAT, A.K.A, "THE CLEANER".
IT WILL LICK THE MILK-SICLE,
SLOWLY CAUSING IT TO SHRINK,
PERPETUATING THE HANGING.
CAT WILL THEN LAP UP PUDDLE,
LEAVING NO EVIDENCE OF
MILK CUBE'S EXISTENCE.

REALLY MURDER BY CAT (THAT WAS REALLY MURDER BY ME)

④ SUICIDE NOTE WRITTEN BY "KELLY DONAHUE" TO
   COMPLETE THE AWESOME MIRAGE THAT THIS WAS
   ALL A SUICIDE INSTEAD OF A CAREFULLY
   ORCHESTRATED DEATH ATTACK TO THE DEATH.

Dear World,
I'm sorry I bored you
for all these years.
Please forget I ever
existed.
Fuck, even this note
is super boring.
I suck.

Yours truly,

Kelly ☺

DEATH PLAN "C": THE I LOOK

START A FIRE IN KELLY DONAHUE'S BUILDING AND SAVE EVERYONE BUT HER, SO SHE BURNS TO DEATH WHILE I GET PRAISED AS A HERO. ("WIN-WIN")

① JAM KELLY DONAHUE'S DOOR LOCKS, PREVENTING EXIT.

② START FIRE.

③ KELLY DONAHUE PASSED OUT ON HER FLOOR.

LIKE A HERO ATTACK

④ BECOME A HERO BY RESCUING 3 OUT OF 4 APARTMENTS.
(HA!)

ME.

ALL THE PEOPLE
I SAVED, 'CAUSE I'M
A HERO.

DEATH PLAN "D": THE CLUE

CONFUSE INVESTIGATORS INTO THINKING THIS WAS
THE DOING OF A BOARDGAME-OBSESSED SERIAL KILLER.

MYSTERY MURDER

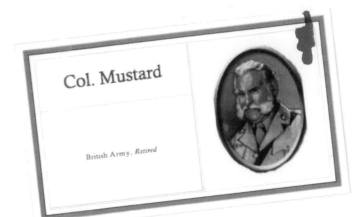

Col. Mustard

British Army, *Retired*

① COLONEL MUSTARD.

② IN THE LIBRARY.

③ WITH THE LEAD PIPE.

DEATH PLAN "E": THE HIGH-TECH

TAKE HER OUT MICHAEL BAY-STYLE, LIKE SHE'S SOME TERRORIST WARLORD AND I'M AN EX-C.I.A. DEMOLITIONS EXPERT WITH NOTHING TO LIVE FOR BUT WHISKEY AND REVENGE.

① RIG HER CELL PHONE WITH EXPLOSIVES. (NOTE: EXPLOSIVES NOT DRAWN TO SCALE.)

② CALL HER # FROM AN OUT-OF-STATE PAYPHONE. (PREFERABLY MONTANA. I HEAR IT'S BEAUTIFUL.)

BLOCKBUSTER SPY-MOVIE ATTACK

③ KABOOM!

THE FIGHT WAS DESTINED FOR GREATNESS, AND YOU'VE
RUINED IT. AND YOU KNOW WHAT, THAT'S TOTALLY FINE.
YOU'RE NOT WORTHY OF BEING LINKED TO SOMETHING
THIS EPIC. IN FACT, I DON'T EVEN **WANT** TO DESTROY
YOU ANYMORE. THAT WOULD JUST PUT YOU OUT OF YOUR
MISERY. I'M NOT GONNA DO YOU THE FAVOR OF
DR. KEVORKIAN-ING YOUR PAINFULLY BORING EXISTENCE.
I MIGHT EVEN BUY YOU SOME ONE-A-DAY VITAMIN
SUPPLEMENTS AND A GYM MEMBERSHIP TO MAKE SURE
YOUR PATHETIC ASS STICKS AROUND ON THIS PLANET AS
LONG AS POSSIBLE, DROWNING IN A SEA OF DULLNESS
AND MEDIOCRITY WITH YOUR TWILIGHT BOOKS AND
YOUR BOCA BURGER MEATLESS PATTIES AND YOUR
GODDAMN DAVE MATTHEWS BAND CDS.

KELLY DONAHUE, YOU DON'T DESERVE "THE FIGHT"
AND YOU DON'T DESERVE ME.

FUCK YOU. <u>LIVE FOREVER</u>!

— MARK

9/28/11

HAVE YOU EVER WOKEN UP ONE MORNING
AND THEN QUIT YOUR JOB AND THEN
BEFORE YOU LEFT THE OFFICE YOU PULLED
OUT A PIECE OF PUTRID, ROTTING SALMON
AND THEN YOU CAREFULLY BURIED IT IN
THE LINING OF THE COAT OF A COWORKER
THAT YOU USED TO WANNA FIGHT TO THE
DEATH BUT THEN YOU CALLED IT OFF
CAUSE SHE'S A WORTHLESS CHEATING
WHOREFACE? I HAVE.

BOARDING PASS

2 027 7460377622 0

EN4FQO

▲DELTA
SVARTZ / MARK

SEAT
26E
ZONE 4

TA03B35Y

CLASS **T**   ORIGIN **NYC-KENNEDY**   DEPARTS **510P**

FLIGHT **DL31**   DATE **30SEPT**   COACH   DESTINATION **SEATTLE**

OPERATED BY
DELTA AIR LINES INC

DEPARTURE GATE **29**   **SUBJECT TO CHANGE**

JFK04FD33/X1

9/30/11

GOT ON A PLANE TO SEATTLE TODAY. MET A
FEW INTERESTING PEOPLE. (SOME OF THEM ARE
FOREIGN-LOOKING.) THERE WAS THIS ONE GIRL
WHO SAID "HEY" IN THE AISLE. ALL I KNOW
ABOUT HER IS THAT:

① HER NAME IS **BETH ERIKSON.**

② SHE SITS IN SEAT 26D.

③ AND I VOW TO PHYSICALLY
DEFEAT HER IN A PHYSICAL
FIGHT TO THE DEATH.
PHYSICALLY !

OH... DELTA HAS FREE PRETZELS. I LIKE IT.

About the Author

Mark Svartz is an author, artist, and award-winning advertising creative. Like most kids who were born and raised in Brooklyn, his lifelong dream was to write a book called *I Hate You, Kelly Donahue.* Amazingly, he is the only one who succeeded. The others are all failures.

This is Mark's first book and to make sure that people find it online, he will now mention random popular terms that will show up in searches: Lady Gaga; Obama; porn; Justin Bieber; Twitter; nude celebs; Oprah; kittens; boobs.

Mark currently lives in New York City and he thinks you are all awesome.